Sugar Gliders

The Complete Sugar Glider Care Guide

Sandy Duncan

www.SugarGliderCare.net

Copyright Notice

First Printing, 2012

ISBN-13: 978-1475080339

ISBN-10: 1475080336

Printed in the United States of America

Contents

Introduction

As sugar gliders have become more and more popular as pets, there has been a lot of information posted online, but much of it is unreliable. As a sugar glider owner, I have done hours of research online and found it to be very frustrating at first because it is hard to know which websites to trust. I have compiled all the reliable information I have found into this book to save you the time and frustration.

Based on my own experiences and consultations with several veterinarians over the years, I have eventually been able to discern the good information from the bad.

Ultimately, you should trust your gut when it comes to judging which information is correct, but it can be difficult to sort it all out in the beginning.

I will warn you that a lot of information online that looks like it comes from official and reliable sources is actually misleading and sometimes harmful. This false information is put out by mill breeders who breed sugar gliders solely to make a profit and do not care about the welfare of the animal.

Although sugar gliders make wonderful pets, they are exotic animals and have specific needs that must be met in order to stay happy and healthy. As a sugar glider owner, you must be educated and prepared to cater to these special needs. Although it is not difficult to care for a sugar glider, it is a big responsibility and requires a major commitment.

This book will cover the important things you need to know about caring for sugar gliders. If you are thinking about getting one or more sugar gliders, this book will help you decide if it is the right pet for you and whether this type of commitment will fit into your lifestyle. It will also prepare you to make the right decisions in caring for your gliders should you decide to get them.

This book will also be helpful for those who already own one or more sugar gliders and are looking for some guidance on how to properly care for these animals. There is a lot of information out there and it can be confusing at times trying to figure it all out. This guide organizes all the information for you and presents the best practices when it comes to caring for your glider.

Chapter 1: Basic Information About Sugar Gliders

The sugar glider (*Petaurus breviceps*) is a marsupial that comes from Australia, Tasmania, Papua New Guinea, and Indonesia. Sugar gliders first became popular as pets in the United States in the early 1990s. Most of the gliders that are bred and sold in the United States today were originally imported from Indonesia and are now bred in captivity.

Sugar gliders get their name from their love of sweet foods such as sap and nectar and their ability to glide through the air, similar to a flying squirrel. They are nocturnal, which means that they sleep during the day and are active at night. In the wild, they sleep in nests in the hollows of trees during the daytime and emerge at night to search for food.

The females carry their young, called joeys, in a pouch. After a gestation period of fifteen to seventeen days, the joey will crawl into its mother's pouch where it will further mature. The joey attaches to a nipple, where it will stay for around sixty to seventy days.

The father also plays an important role in raising a young joey once it has left the pouch. While the joey is still young, it cannot regulate its own body temperature, so the father will stay in the nest to keep the joey warm whenever the mother has to leave the nest.

Sugar gliders are omnivores, and in the wild, they eat a varied diet of tree sap, nectar, pollen, acacia gum, insects and other arthropods, lizards, baby birds, small vertebrates, and eggs. They are sap suckers and will use their teeth to scrape the bark off of Eucalyptus and other trees to get to the sap. They also suck the nectar and pollen out of flowers.

Sugar gliders are very social animals and live in colonies of seven or more in the wild. They are territorial animals and will mark their territory with scent glands, saliva, and urine. The males have scent glands on the top of their heads which look like bald spots and also have scent glands on their chest.

An alpha male will mark the other members of the colony by rubbing his forehead under their chins. They recognize members of their own colony by scent and will often attack or even kill gliders from other colonies.

Male gliders are usually larger than females. The average weight for an adult male is 115-160 grams, and the average weight for an adult female is 95-135 grams. They are approximately 5-7 inches in length from the tip of the nose to the base of the tail, and the tail is usually the same length as the body. They use their tails as a rudder to steer while gliding through the air and also to carry small items back to their nests.

Sugar gliders can glide through the air thanks to their gliding membrane, called the patagium. It extends from the fifth finger to the first toe and stretches out like a parachute when they glide through the air. In the wild, sugar gliders can glide up to 150 feet from tree to tree in search of food.

There are several different color variations, but the most common is a silvery grey back with a cream colored chest and belly. They have a black stripe running from the top of the head to the lower back and a silver and black bushy tail. A healthy glider will have soft and silky fur.

Sugar gliders have 40 teeth and it is important to note that unlike rodents, their teeth will not continue to grow. You should never float or file a gliders teeth because it would cause permanent pain and difficulty eating.

In the wild, sugar gliders have a lifespan of 4-7 years, but they live much longer in captivity. The potential lifespan in captivity is 12-15 years when cared for properly.

Chapter 2: Deciding Whether To Get A Sugar Glider

If you are thinking about getting one or more sugar gliders as pets, you should do thorough research beforehand. They are high maintenance pets, and in order to take proper care of them, you will need to be educated about their special needs. In this section, I will discuss some of the most important things that you need to be aware of before taking on sugar gliders as pets.

Unfortunately, there are sugar glider mills that have operations across the country peddling sugar gliders at mall kiosks, flea markets, trade shows, and state fairs. They market sugar gliders as easy pets so they can make a quick buck. They will put on demonstrations showing adult gliders who are well socialized to lure people in. They may even have somebody hold up a glider and have it glide to another person's shoulder to draw people in.

These mill operations breed thousands of gliders and make millions of dollars selling them to people who buy on impulse. Sugar gliders should never be bought on impulse. They are actually high maintenance pets, and unsuspecting potential owners should be aware of this.

Many people have been fooled into believing that they do not require much effort to take care of. Although caring for sugar gliders is not difficult in itself, they do require a lot of specialized care which can be difficult for people who do not have the time to devote to them.

If you happen to see sugar gliders being sold at the mall, flea market, trade shows, or state fairs, please be wary of the information they give out. These people have a motive in convincing you that sugar gliders are easy to take care of because they want you to purchase one.

Questions To Consider Before Deciding To Get A Sugar Glider

1. Are sugar gliders legal in your state?

Sugar gliders are not legal in every state. Each state has different laws when it comes to owning sugar gliders, so you will need to verify that it is legal to own them in your home state. Some states also require that you purchase from a USDA licensed breeder, so it is important to find out what your state requires.

In addition, some cities have laws forbidding ownership as well. For example, it is legal to own a sugar glider in the state of New York, but it is illegal in the five boroughs of New York City.

Here are two websites that can help you determine whether sugar gliders are legal in your state:

http://www.sugarglider.com/gliderpedia/index.asp?Laws

http://www.angelfire.com/nb/sugarglider/stateres.html

Be sure to verify any information you find online by calling your local city and state agencies.

2. If you rent your home, are sugar gliders permitted by your landlord?

Some buildings and landlords will not allow you to have exotic pets in your home. If you rent, you should check with your landlord ahead of time to make sure it is permitted to keep a sugar glider.

3. Are you willing to commit to owning sugar gliders for 15 years?

Gliders can potentially live up to 15 years in captivity, so you must be sure that you can make a longterm commitment. If you know you will be having significant changes in your life in the next 15 years, make sure a sugar glider will still fit into your changing lifestyle.

4. Are you willing to get at least 2 sugar gliders?

Sugar gliders are very social animals and will not thrive if they do not have at least one companion. I would highly recommend getting at least two gliders to keep each other company. It is true that you can get one sugar glider and it will be okay, but it may not thrive if you cannot spend enough time with it. As you would be its only companion, you will have to spend a lot of time with it, and that is not always possible for every owner.

5. Can you afford to take care of sugar gliders?

Sugar gliders are not cheap pets. An average grey glider from a reputable breeder may cost around $150 - $200. Also keep in mind that it is much better to get at least two. If you get one that is a rarer color, they can be more expensive. Then, you must consider the cost of the cage, which can be in the range of $120 to $400 depending on the size.

You will need to get an exercise wheel, which costs about $50. You will also need other things for the cage, including hanging pouches, hammocks, food and water bowls, and toys. Gliders require a variety of toys to stay mentally stimulated.

There is also the cost of veterinarian care. Veterinarians who deal with exotic pets may charge more than the average veterinarian.

6. Is there an exotic pet veterinarian in your area that can treat sugar gliders?

It can be difficult finding a veterinarian that deals with sugar gliders. You should locate a veterinarian in your area before you purchase a sugar glider. It is also a good idea to find a backup veterinarian in case the first one becomes unavailable. Additionally, you should make sure to locate an emergency veterinarian that can treat sugar gliders in case you have an emergency late at night when the regular veterinarian is closed.

7. Can you find somebody to take care of your sugar gliders when you are away from home?

You cannot leave sugar gliders unsupervised if you will be away from home. You should have somebody you trust to take care of them in the event that you will be away from home.

8. Are you willing to ensure that they eat a balanced diet of protein and fresh or frozen fruits and vegetables?

Sugar gliders have specific dietary needs in order to stay healthy. It is not true that you can just feed them dry pellets and a slice of apple. There are several different diets that are acceptable for sugar gliders, but they will all require that you provide a variety of fresh or frozen fruits and vegetables.

It is very important that gliders get enough calcium, and you also need to make sure their foods have the proper calcium to phosphorous ratio of 2:1. If sugar gliders do not get enough calcium, they can get Hind Leg Paralysis (HLP).

9. Do you have enough time to care for your sugar gliders properly?

Sugar gliders are not low maintenance pets and require a large time commitment. You will need to bond with them during the day while they are sleeping, allow them to play for at least two hours out of their cage, prepare their food, clean their cage, and more. If you only have one glider, it is even more important to spend a lot of time bonding and playing with your glider.

10. Will it work with your schedule to have a nocturnal pet?

Sugar gliders are nocturnal, so they will be up all night and sleep during the day. You may have to stay up later than normal to let them out to play for a couple hours and feed them while they are awake at night. If you plan to keep them in your bedroom, you should be aware that they will be up all night possibly making noise that could disturb your sleep. They may bark, run in their wheel, or jump around in their cage.

11. Are you okay with having a pet who may be messy and smelly?

Sugar gliders are messy eaters and will throw their food around. They may also mark their territory with urine. You will have to be diligent about keeping their cage and other belongings clean.

Depending on what diet you have them on, they may be smelly. Some gliders will be smellier than others depending on how strong their scent glands are. Males who have not been neutered will be the smelliest due to their scent glands. Once a male has been neutered, the scent glands will not be as strong.

12. Will you mind having a pet that cannot be potty trained?

Sugar gliders cannot really be potty trained. They will pee and poop on you, and if you let them roam free, they will pee and poop wherever and whenever they need to. There are some things you can do to motivate them to go to the bathroom when they have just woken up before letting them play, but there is no guarantee that they will not go again later.

13. Can you provide a safe environment for you sugar gliders?

There are many things in your home that can be harmful to a sugar glider. Gliders have opposable thumbs and are known to be quite the little escape artists. Even if you think they are secure in their cages, you should always make sure to glider proof your home.

The most common cause of accidental deaths to gliders is drowning in toilets. You must be careful to leave toilet seats down and make sure there is no water they can fall into anywhere in your home. Although they can swim, they will not be able to climb out if they fall into a toilet, and then they can become exhausted and drown.

Another potential harm to sugar gliders is other household pets. It is best to keep your gliders separated from other household pets such as cats and dogs, because you do not know how your other animals will react to your glider. It is an unnecessary risk to try to bond your sugar glider to your other pets, because animals are unpredictable.

If you have young children, you should always supervise them while they are handling the gliders. Gliders are fragile and could easily get injured by a child who does not know how to properly handle them.

Some common house plants are toxic to sugar gliders, so you will have to be careful to check and make sure any accessible house plants are safe for your glider to be around.

Toxic chemicals can also be harmful to gliders, so it is important to keep any household cleaners or other items that contain toxic chemicals away from your gliders. You should also be careful about any topical medications or chemicals you put on your body. Gliders will lick you, or chemicals may rub onto their fur when you touch them and get ingested when they groom themselves.

Before you decide to get a pet sugar glider, you should ask yourself all of these questions and take some time to think about whether you will be able to handle such a commitment. Sugar glider rescues all over the country are full of gliders who have been abandoned by people who bought them on impulse.

If you cannot honestly say that you will be able to meet all of their special needs and deal with some of the drawbacks, then you should not become a sugar glider owner.

Of course, if you are willing to be a responsible sugar glider owner, they make wonderful pets.   They are loyal and loving companions and will provide you with hours of joy and amusement.   They are extremely intelligent animals and are fun to watch as they play and explore their environment.

If you put in the time to bond with them, they can form a very strong bond with you and become amazing companions.   It is fun to carry them around on you wherever you go and most people will not have a clue that you have a tiny critter with you.

Chapter 3: Where To Get Sugar Gliders

I f you decide to make the commitment to get one or more sugar gliders as pets, you will need to do some research on where to acquire them. There are a few good options you can consider as well as some places to avoid.

Adopting sugar gliders from a local rescue is one option you can consider. There are sugar gliders in rescues all across the country in need of a good home, and you could help save them by providing a loving and caring home. Rescuing gliders is also one way to be sure that you are not supporting sugar glider mills.

Another good option is to purchase your gliders from a reputable local breeder who offers after-sale support. By purchasing locally, you can visit the breeder check it out and make sure they provide a clean and safe environment. You can also check to see that the gliders are all healthy and well cared for.

Another option is to find a breeder on the Internet, but this is not recommended. Some breeders will ship sugar gliders to you, but they have to take proper care that it is done safely. The problem is that there is no way to see the breeding facilities or meet the parents. Buying on the Internet is also risky because sellers are not regulated under the Animal Welfare Act.

Signs Of A Good Breeder

1. U.S. Department of Agriculture (USDA) License

One thing you can check for is to see if a breeder has a USDA license. Although having a USDA license is a good thing, unfortunately it is not a reliable indicator of a good breeder, so you will have to investigate further. On the flip side, just because a breeder does not have a USDA license does not mean they are a bad breeder. Only breeders who have more than three breeding females are required to obtain a USDA license.

2. Clean facility and healthy gliders

A good breeder will let you come see their facilities so you can make sure they provide a clean environment for their gliders. They will also let you meet their gliders to make sure they are healthy and well cared for. Make sure the cages are big enough and that they have plenty of toys.

If a breeder makes excuses and will not let you see their facilities, you should not trust them. Good breeders will not to try to hide anything from you.

3. They recommend a balanced diet

Ask potential breeders what diet they recommend. A good breeder will always be honest and recommend a balanced diet of protein and fresh or frozen fruits and vegetables.

4. Joeys are separated from the parents no sooner than 8-12 weeks out of pouch

A good breeder will never separate joeys from the parents earlier than eight to twelve weeks out of pouch (OOP). Make sure they count from the out of pouch date and not the actual birth date.

5. They offer after-sale support

Good breeders will feel an obligation to their joeys, even after they have gone home with a new owner. Many will be available for 24/7 support if you need anything.

6. They offer a health guarantee and provide lineage

Make sure to ask about a breeders health guarantee as many good ones will offer a one month guarantee. They should also be able to provide lineage on any gliders they breed to avoid inbreeding. It is a good idea to meet both parents of the sugar glider you will be taking home, or at least the mother.

A good breeder will provide you with an adoption contract that explains their responsibilities to you, the health guarantee, and their return policy.

7. They are experienced and can provide references

Ask how long they have been in business to see how much experience they have breeding gliders. Good breeders will also be able to provide you with references if you ask.

8. They are happy to answer any questions and also have questions for you

Good breeders will not mind answering your questions. Many will also have questions for you too because they want to make sure their joeys go to a good home. If it seems like they only care about money and not the welfare of their gliders, avoid them.

Where to Avoid Getting Your Sugar Gliders

You should avoid getting sugar gliders from mall kiosks, flea markets, trade shows, state fairs, and other places that encourage impulse buying. These locations are usually set up by mill breeders who encourage impulse buying by people who are not educated about sugar gliders.

Sadly, many of the gliders that are sold by mills are not in good health or may have been separated from their mothers too soon. Many of the gliders that are bought on impulse also end up being abandoned, sold on craigslist, or sent to rescue shelters because the owners were not prepared to take care of such a high maintenance pet.

There are some exceptions, but you should also avoid pet stores because they usually get their gliders from mills. Many pet stores are not knowledgeable about how to care for sugar gliders and will often mislead people to believe that they are easier to care for than they really are.

Pet stores are usually closed in the evening so they rarely handle sugar gliders at night when they are most active and needing attention. Pet stores are also loud and can be scary and stressful to a small sugar glider. It may be more challenging to bond with them after they have been in a stressful environment.

There are a few good pet stores out there, so if you think you have found a reputable one, make sure to ask a lot of questions to make sure they are knowledgeable about sugar gliders and take proper care of them.

Signs Of An Irresponsible Seller

1. A bunch of joeys crammed into one cage

Avoid any seller who comes to a public place with a group of joeys all crowded together in one cage. They do not know one joey from the next and cannot tell you anything about the personalities or characteristics of the individual joeys.

2. Not allowed to meet the joey before you buy

Avoid any seller who will not let you see the sugar glider before you purchase it. It is important to be able to handle a sugar glider and play with it before you buy it so you can see if it has been handled and tamed by the breeder.

3. Recommends sugar gliders as easy, low maintenance, and inexpensive pets

Avoid any seller who says sugar gliders are easy, low maintenance, or inexpensive pets. As explained already, sugar gliders are high maintenance pets and are not cheap. Anybody who tells you otherwise is probably trying to push a sale and does not care about the welfare of the sugar gliders.

4. Recommends sugar gliders for children

Avoid any seller who uses a sales method that targets children, for example, characterizing sugar gliders as good starter pets for kids. Sugar gliders are not good pets for young children and require a responsible adult to take care of them.

5. Claims sugar gliders will get along with your other pets

Avoid any seller who claims that sugar gliders will get along with your other household pets. Some people will claim that your dog or cat will not attack a glider because they do not smell like rodents, but this is not true. Cats and dogs will go after small animals who run or move quickly, and your sugar glider is no exception.

6. Recommends getting a single glider

Avoid any seller who tells you that a single glider will be alright without another glider companion for its entire life. In some cases, a single glider may do fine, but it is much better to have at least one companion.

7. Recommends a small cage

Avoid any seller who recommends a small bird cage. Sugar gliders are arboreal, which means they spend a lot of their time in the tree tops. They need a tall cage to jump and climb, so the taller the better. The smallest cage size should be 36"H x 24"L x 24"W, or 40"H x 21"L x 21"W.

Some sellers say that joeys need a smaller cage because they are young, and it is easier bond with them because it will be easier to catch them in a smaller cage. This is not true. You should get the same size cage for joeys that you would for adults.

8. Recommends a heat rock

Avoid any seller who tells you to use a heat rock or tries to sell you a heat rock with a cage. Joeys that are fully weaned and ready to leave the parents can regulate their own temperature and do not need a separate heat source. If a seller recommends a heat rock, chances are they are selling a joey that is too young to be separated from its parents.

9. Requires you to follow their diet

Avoid any seller who tells you that you have to feed a specific diet. There are many approved diets for sugar gliders which will be discussed later in this book. Be especially wary of anybody who tells you to feed a mostly pellet diet with a slice of apple and a slice of wheat bread. Sugar gliders need a variety of protein and fresh or frozen fruits and vegetables.

10. Claims gliders can be potty trained

Avoid any seller who tells you that gliders will not pee or poop on you or says they can be potty trained. You can consider yourself a moving toilet because sugar gliders like to mark their owners and will poop whenever and wherever they need to. They can be encouraged to go after waking up, but that does not mean they will not go again later.

11. Claims sugar gliders will not bite, or not hard enough to draw blood

Avoid any seller who says sugar gliders will not bite or will not bite hard enough to draw any blood. When sugar gliders get scared or are provoked in any way, they will bite to defend themselves.

12. Recommends using physical force to stop biting

Avoid any seller who recommends using physical force to train or discipline a glider to stop biting. Gliders are small and using physical force could injure or kill them. There are other better ways to stop a glider from biting. One way is to mimic the "pssst" sound that gliders make to each other when a behavior is not tolerated.

13. Claims sugar glider rescues do not exist and are a scam

Avoid any seller who claims that sugar glider rescues do not exist and are really a scam. There are glider rescues all across the country that take in abandoned and sick gliders who were originally sold to impulse buyers by mills.

14. Claims sugar gliders only bond when they are young

Avoid any seller who says sugar gliders will only bond when they are very young, from 8 to 12 weeks old. Many adult gliders bond very well to their owners as well.

How To Know If A Sugar Glider Is Old Enough To Bring Home

From eight to twelve weeks out of pouch, a sugar glider is usually ready to be weaned from its parents. You do not want to buy a sugar glider that has been taken away from its parents too soon because it is better to let the weaning process occur naturally.

Sugar gliders learn a lot of behaviors from their parents, such as how to eat and how to behave according to a pecking order in the colony. Taking them away too soon can cause behavioral problems and affect them for the rest of their lives. In addition to potential behavioral problems, sugar gliders who are removed from their parents too soon also have a higher risk of dying early on or having health issues.

Hopefully you have found a breeder that you can trust, but some sellers may not always be honest about the age of a joey. There are signs you can look for to determine whether a joey is too young to be separated from its parents.

Signs That A Joey Is Too Young To Be Separated From Its Parents

1. Smooth tail

If a joey has a smooth tail with fur that lays flat, it is probably under four weeks old out of pouch and definitely too young to be taken from its parents. You want to look for a full and fluffy tail.

2. Crying

A joey who cries when put on a strange surface is crying for its parents and not ready to be weaned.

3. Riding on another glider

If a joey rides on another glider's back, it is too young to be weaned. A weaned joey will never ride around on another glider's back.

4. Does not walk properly

If a glider is not sure footed, does not walk steady, or is sprawled out on all fours, it is too young to be weaned.

5. Smaller than the width of your hand

A sugar glider that is smaller than the width of an average sized hand may be too young. The body length, not including the tail, should be about the width of your hand, or slightly longer.

How to Make Sure a Sugar Glider is Healthy

Here are some signs of an unhealthy glider to watch out for:

1. Wet looking, greasy, sticky, or matted fur

A healthy glider will have soft, thick, clean fur. Fur that looks wet, greasy, sticky, or matted could be signs of a parasite or bacterial infection, or unhealthy living conditions.

2. Dull eyes or discharge

A healthy glider will have bright, clear eyes that are full of life. An unhealthy joey may have eyes that have discharge, or they may appear dull, blueish in color, or irritated looking.

3. Ribs showing

Joeys that are underweight or have ribs showing can be sick or dehydrated.

4. Lethargic

A healthy glider will be active and alert, so any joey that looks lethargic or unaware of things going on around them could be sick.

5. Wet tail or poop matted to tail

A joey that has a wet tail or poop matted to the tail is not grooming itself and may be sick. It could also be a sign that it is too young to be away from its parents and may not have learned to groom itself yet.

6. Flattened or dry ears

Ears that are constantly flattened and will not perk up when spoken to, or ears that are dry and scaly could be signs of illness.

If you see any of these signs or anything else that makes you suspicious, do not hesitate to point it out to the breeder. Ask as many questions as you can about the health of the glider and do not buy from a breeder who cannot answer your questions satisfactorily.

Although you may feel sorry for a sick glider, it is important not to buy one because it will only support the breeder and help keep them in business. It does not help sick gliders in the long run to support the businesses who sell them.

It is best to report them to the American Society for the Prevention of Cruelty to Animals (ASPCA) or the Better Business Bureau (BBB). You can also ask for their USDA license number and verify that they are licensed. If they are not, you can report them to the USDA.

Chapter 4: Setting Up The Cage

Before you bring your sugar gliders home, you should have a cage set up for them. The minimum size for a pair of gliders should be 36"H x 24"L x 24"W or 40"H x 21"L x 21"W. The taller the cage, the better it is for your gliders, because they love to jump and climb.

Look for a cage that has horizontal bars spaced no more than half an inch apart. Make sure there are horizontal bars so your gliders can get a foothold for climbing.

It is important not to get galvanized wires because it can be harmful to gliders. Look for a cage that is made of PVC coated wires, powder coated wires, or wrought iron. It is best not to have any parts of the cage made of wood because it will soak up urine and smell bad. Some woods are also toxic to gliders, such as walnut and cedar.

It may not be easy to find a cage that is made specifically for sugar gliders in your area. Some people get birdcages, but they are not always the best for gliders. They can easily escape from the small doors that are made for birds, so you would need to use zip ties to secure the doors. It may also be hard to find a birdcage that has the right bar spacing.

There are a lot of places online where you can purchase a cage that is made specifically for gliders. Ebay is a great place to look.

Another option is to make a cage out of PVC pipes and wire mesh. People take this route because it is often cheaper and allows you to customize the cage to your liking. You can find different cage designs online to serve as a guideline.

Drop Pan

Make sure there is a removable tray underneath the bottom of the cage to catch urine and feces. You can line the tray with newspapers, glider-safe litter, puppy pads, or fleece. Pine and cedar bedding are toxic to gliders, so look for something that is safe for gliders.

There is a litter that is made from recycled newspapers that works well. Puppy pads are also good because they absorb odors well. Some people use fleece because it is inexpensive and can be machine washed. You can shake it clean every day and change it out every few days.

It is important to put the cage in a place where your gliders will be able to see when it is night and day so you do not mess up their biological clock. You also need to make sure the cage is not exposed to direct sunlight, because this can be harmful to your glider's nocturnal eyes.

Elevate your cage if possible because sugar gliders like to be high up off the ground as they spend most of their time up in the tree tops in their natural habitat.

The temperature should be kept at 70 to 90 degrees fahrenheit in order for your gliders to be most comfortable. A good rule of thumb is to keep the room at a temperature at which you would be comfortable. If you are too cold, then your glider is probably too cold as well.

If you need to, you can use a space heater to keep the temperature warmer in the room where you keep your gliders, but it is not necessary if you keep your home around 70 degrees or more.

Food and Water Dishes

You should provide two or even three sources of water in the cage in case something happens to one. Bottles can clog, leak, go empty, or break, so it is smart to have a backup source in the cage in case you do not notice right away.

You can use a water dish, but the water will probably get dirty easily or get contaminated with urine or feces.

Water bottles or water silos that attach to the cage are good options.

Young gliders may not know how to drink out of water bottles, so provide a water dish until they learn. You can add a little apple juice to the water or put a dab of honey or yogurt on the end of the water bottle to motivate your glider to learn how to drink out of the bottle.

For food bowls, you can either use regular food dishes or hanging food bowls. Gliders are messy eaters and often throw their food out of the cage. To contain the mess, you can use a glider kitchen, which is just a container that has a hole in it so your gliders can get inside.

You can cut a hole or archway into a plastic storage container and sand down any sharp edges. Just turn the container upside down over the food bowls to provide a shelter to contain the mess. Pet igloos also work well and can usually be found at your local pet store.

Cage Pouch Or Nesting Box

You will need to provide a nesting box or cage pouch for your glider to sleep in. In the wild, sugar gliders sleep in nests high up in the hollows of trees, so the pouch or nesting box will provide that same sense of security.

Fleece is a great material for pouches because it does not fray and gliders will not get their nails stuck in it. It is also best to get a pouch with hidden seams because a glider's feet can also get caught in the seams.

It is a good idea to have several fleece pouches on hand to rotate for cleaning because they can get smelly. If a pouch ever rips or gets a hole, replace it immediately because gliders can get stuck or injured.

You can purchase cage sets that come with a pouch and hammock, as well as other things such as vines, bridges, and tunnels. Cage sets are usually made out of fleece and can be washed easily. It is a good idea to get a few cage sets so you can rotate them for cleaning.

You can also add perches or branches to your cage for your glider to climb on. If you add fresh branches, be aware that some woods are toxic to gliders and make sure that any wood you use is free of pesticides.

Wood also absorbs urine and will eventually get smelly. If your glider likes to chew, the wood will also need to be replaced when the bark has been stripped off or the wood becomes dry and brittle because splinters can be dangerous. You can also get fake branches that are easier to keep clean.

Exercise Wheel

Another must have item for your cage is a wheel because gliders love to run and jump in them, and it is a fun way for your glider to get some exercise. Do not get a wire wheel made for hamsters because those can cause foot injuries to gliders and they are not the correct size. Also avoid wheels with a center bar/axle because those can cause tail injuries if your glider's tail gets caught around the bar.

There are several glider-safe wheels available to choose from. One popular wheel among sugar glider owners is the Stealth Wheel (pictured below) because it is extremely quiet and easy to clean.

It was designed specifically for sugar gliders, so it does not have a center bar. It is safer and provides more room for them to leap and run. You can get the stealth wheel here: http://www.atticworx.com.

Toys

Sugar gliders are curious and playful animals, so it is important to provide them with a variety of toys to keep them stimulated.

Bird toys are available at pet stores and work well for gliders, but make sure there are not any small parts that could be a choking hazard. Baby and toddler toys are usually good for gliders as well.

It is not recommended to use cat toys because many contain catnip, which is toxic to gliders.

Some popular children's toys that gliders love are Barrel of Monkeys and Toy Soldiers.

You can get plastic chains to hang from the top of the cage that your gliders can play with. Foraging toys that you can use to hide food and treats are popular as well because gliders forage for food in the wild. You can make foraging toys by filling a container with cut straws or strips of fleece, or use a easter egg that opens up to hide treats.

You can get creative and make fun toys for your gliders. For an easy toy to make, put straws through a wiffle ball to create a fun game for your gliders. Watch them have fun pulling the straws out, and they might even carry the straws off in their tail and take it into their nesting box.

Another fun idea is to braid fleece into a rope and string wiffle balls through it. This makes a very nice climbing rope for your glider.

You can also decorate the cage with fake plants or leafy vines, but make sure there are no wires or glue on them. Gliders love to pluck the leaves and nest with them.

Remember to rotate toys regularly so your glider does not get bored. Rotating toys will also give you a chance to clean them.

Chapter 5: Glider Proofing Your Home

I t would be wise to glider proof your house before you bring your new glider home. At a minimum, you will need to glider proof one room in your home where you will be letting them out to play.

Even if you only plan to let your glider play in one room, it is still a good idea to glider proof your entire house because they are known to escape from their cages thanks to their opposable thumbs and clever disposition. They are quite intelligent and curious animals, so they can get into a lot of trouble quickly if you have not taken the necessary precautions.

It is a good idea to make sure the door to the room your sugar gliders are in is always closed in case they were to escape from their cage. If there is room under the door for them to squeeze through, you can line it with a towel or get a draft guard to close up the gap. Even a gap as small as half an inch can be big enough for them to squeeze through.

I will cover some of the most common things to watch out for when glider proofing your home, but you should be aware that this is not a complete list. This list is a good guideline, but you should also go through your home carefully and look for any potential hazards to your sugar glider that may not be on the list.

1. Keep toilet lids down and cover or remove standing water

It is extremely important to always keep the toilet lid down and remove or cover standing water in sinks, vases, fish tanks, etc. As you can see from the picture, a glider will even climb into a water glass, so be careful not to leave any liquids out.

Even though gliders can swim, once they fall into a toilet or other source of standing water, they cannot grab onto the smooth surface to climb back out, so they end up getting exhausted and drowning.

Some toilet seats sit high up off the rim, so you should get down to eye level with the seat and check to see if there is any space between the rim and the seat. If there is more than a 3/8" gap, you may have to replace the toilet seat because your glider may be able to squeeze through. Some people use duct tape to close the gaps and prevent gliders from squeezing through, but that is not the most practical solution.

If there are other people living with you, it is a good idea to put a sign on the toilet reminding them to close the lid after use.

Some sugar glider owners will make a ladder out of hardware cloth that hooks onto the side of the toilet bowl and extends down far enough for them to grab onto to climb out in case they fall in.

2. Cover or plug drains

Make sure all drains are covered or plugged securely so that your glider cannot get in. It is especially important to plug the kitchen sink so they do not get into the garbage disposal.

3. Close gaps in walls, doors, windows, and cabinets

Look closely at cabinets in your bathroom and kitchen for small holes that your glider could climb into. Check for spaces between cabinets, or holes between the cabinet and the wall. Feel underneath the cabinets and counter tops because there are sometimes holes that can only be seen from underneath.

You should also check for even the tiniest holes in the walls. Check around plumbing because there are often gaps in the wall where plumbing is installed. Also check around baseboards and window frames for small gaps.

If you have pocket doors, check underneath the brackets under the door to see if there are holes where a glider could crawl into the wall. Metal framed shower doors are hollow and may be open at the top leaving a space for your glider to climb in.

4. Close windows

Make sure your windows are shut because gliders can chew through the screen and get out. Even if the window is only cracked, they can still squeeze underneath.

5. Close off fireplaces

Make sure fireplaces are completely sealed off. If a glider were to get into your fireplace, they could easily climb the brick chimney and get outside.

6. Cover air and heating vents

Make sure gliders cannot get into the air ducts by keeping air vents covered. Alternatively, you can get aluminum screening or hardware cloth to line the inside of vents so that your gliders cannot squeeze through and air will still flow out.

7. Cover radiators, baseboard heaters, space heaters, air conditioners, humidifiers, fans, etc.

Inspect any heating or cooling devices in your home for holes that your glider could fit through. You can line any vents or holes with aluminum screening or hardware cloth so your gliders cannot squeeze through and air still flows out.

8. Close off access to washer and dryer

It is best to keep your laundry room closed at all times. Washers and dryers usually have space underneath where a glider could fit. The dryer is also vented to the outside, so you definitely do not want your glider getting access to the dryer vent. If your glider is out of its cage, make sure to check your laundry before loading it into the washer because gliders like to curl up in your clothes.

9. Keep ceiling fans off and close up any holes in the base

Ceiling fans are very appealing to a glider because they love to climb up onto them and glide down. Make sure your fan is off whenever your glider is out of its cage. Check the base of the fan for any holes that are big enough for your glider to get stuck in.

10. Close any gaps in furniture

Check underneath furniture and make sure the bottom is sealed. If there are any gaps in furniture, gliders will climb inside. Above is a picture of my glider hanging out in a dresser drawer after climbing in through the back.

Recliners or pull-out sofa beds are a hazard because they can crawl inside and get caught up in the hinges. They will also climb into dressers, couches, mattresses, and box springs if there are any openings.

11. Cover electrical outlets and electrical cords

Cover all electrical outlets with child safety plugs. Gliders can stick their tongues into open outlets and get electrocuted. Remove or cover electrical cords and wires because some gliders like to chew on the cords.

12. Cover electronics, appliances, and vacuums

Gliders are known to climb inside televisions, VCRs, printers, vacuum hoses, toasters, you name it. If you have any electronics or appliances that have openings, make sure they are out of reach or cover them up.
Gliders can also do things like pop battery covers off of remote controls and pop keys off of keyboards, so be careful to remove anything that is in their reach that you do not want them messing with. You can think of them as toddlers that you always have to keep an eye on.

13. Remove any toxic house plants

Some house plants are toxic to sugar gliders. Make sure any plants you have in your home are safe. Gliders will chew up your plants and scatter the dirt, so it is easier to just get rid of them entirely or keep them away from your gliders.

You can visit these websites for information on what plants are safe for sugar gliders:

http://www.sugarglider.com/gliderpedia/index.asp? GliderToxicPlants

http://www.moondance-sugargliders.com/sugar_glider_ plant-tree_information.htm

14. Hang pictures with two nails and remove posters

If you have pictures up on the walls, make sure to hang them with two nails because gliders will jump on them and knock them down. They will also jump onto posters and tear them as they fall down clinging onto them.

15. Use non-toxic cleaning products

Be sure to use non-toxic cleaning products because gliders like to lick things. Avoid using toxic chemicals. You can use natural household ingredients such as a vinegar and water solution, lemon juice, or baking soda to clean and disinfect any area your glider has access to.

16. Secure curtain and drapery cords

If your curtains or drapes have a looped cord, it can be a strangulation hazard to your glider. There are ways to secure the cord so it is stationary rather than hanging down where your glider can access it.

17. Prevent access to hot surfaces

Make sure your glider cannot access any hot surfaces. This includes light bulbs, stovetops, ovens, and even faucets that have had hot water running. Make sure to run the cold water last to keep faucets from scalding them.

18. Close off dog or cat doors

If you have a pet door that gives your dog or cat access to the outside, make sure it is closed off if your sugar glider is out of its cage.

19. Keep poisons and toxic materials locked up and out of reach

Make sure you have not left anything sitting around that is poisonous to your glider. This includes bug spray, cleaning solvents, detergents, medications or over the counter drugs, candles, and chocolate.

20. Put lids on trash bins

It is a good idea to get lids for your trash bins in case there are any dangerous materials in the trash.

This is not a complete list, so you will need to check your home for any other potential dangers. Your gliders will probably bring things to your attention, so just keep an eye on them as they explore their environment.

If your glider gets into a space you cannot reach, you can try to coax it out with a treat. It is better to try to get them to come out on their own.

For your glider proofed room, it is a good idea to make a checklist so you can be sure the environment is safe each time you let your gliders out. Always make sure their cage is left open so they can access food and water and nest in there if they want to.

It is also a good idea to leave alternative nesting spots around the room so they have safe places to nest. This will encourage them to nest there instead of looking for unsafe places to get into.

Chapter 6: Diet And Nutrition

What consists of a proper diet for sugar gliders in captivity is a controversial issue. It can be confusing trying to figure it all out because there is a lot of conflicting information out there. Since there are many different acceptable diets, it is important to understand the basic nutritional needs of sugar gliders and what can cause diseases.

Many diseases in sugar gliders are a result of an improper diet, and these can easily be avoided by educating yourself on proper nutrition. In addition to diseases, an improper diet can also cause your glider to smell bad or have dull, cracked, or brittle fur. Sugar gliders who do not get proper nutrition will also have a shorter lifespan.

It is generally accepted that a sugar glider's diet should consist of 50% protein, 25% fruits, and 25% vegetables. For each glider, the correct portions are 2 tablespoons of protein, 1 tablespoon of fruits, and 1 tablespoon of vegetables.

There are many different diets that can be used successfully, and all of them will consist of some source of protein in addition to fresh or frozen fruits and vegetables.

It is extremely important to review whatever diet you choose with your veterinarian to make sure it is nutritionally adequate. Consulting with your veterinarian is always a good idea whenever you make any decisions that will affect the health of your sugar glider.

It is a good idea to follow the breeder's diet at first because sudden changes in diet can be stressful to gliders. If you plan to change your glider's diet at any time, do it gradually and make sure your glider adapts to the new diet successfully.

A proper diet for sugar gliders will consist mainly of fresh food. Any diet that consists mainly of dry pellets, such as a "pellets and apple slice" diet, is not going to have adequate nutrients to keep your glider healthy. Even if pellets were specially formulated for sugar gliders and claim to be a complete and balanced nutritional diet, they are not. If you look at the first few ingredients, they usually contain fillers such as soybean oil, corn meal, or wheat flour.

In addition to containing fillers, pellets are hard and can be rough on a sugar glider's mouth and digestive system. Sugar gliders are sap suckers by nature, so their teeth are designed to strip bark off trees, rather than for chewing, so they can suck out the sap. Since a glider's natural diet consists of wet and juicy foods, they are not adapted to eat dry foods which can become impacted and cause intestinal blockages.

Some people offer dry foods as a "staple" that is available in the cage at all times in case a glider wakes up during the day and wants a little snack to munch on. It is also a way to make sure that adequate amounts of food are offered or can be used as a backup in case you are not able to feed your glider on time one night. It is acceptable to use dry food as a cage staple as long as it is not the main component of your glider's diet.

One crucial element of a sugar glider's diet is maintaining a calcium to phosphorous ratio of 2:1. The calcium to phosphorous ratio is extremely important because too much phosphorous inhibits the absorption of calcium. This can cause a calcium deficiency which weakens the bones, making your glider more susceptible to injuries, metabolic bone disease, and Hind Leg Paralysis (HLP).

It is also important to avoid fatty foods and too many sweet foods because it is not healthy for your glider to be overweight. Fatty foods can also cause partial blindness in gliders because fat deposits build up in the eyes and form a layer over the eye that obstructs vision.

Sugar gliders can be like children, so you may have to use some persuasion to get them to eat a balanced diet. They would pig out on junk food if you let them, so you have to be sure to offer a variety of healthy foods to keep them interested and ration the foods that are not good for them. If your glider develops a favorite food, you may want to ration that as well in order to encourage a more varied diet.

Variety in a sugar glider's diet is very important for both nutritional balance as well as stimulation and prevention of boredom. In the beginning, there may be a lot of trial and error to figure out what your glider will eat because all sugar gliders have individual tastes.

Experimenting with a variety of foods will allow you to figure out what your glider likes while also giving them a properly balanced diet. It does not hurt to keep trying foods even if your glider would not eat them the first time, because their tastes may change day by day.

Since sugar gliders eat at night, you can put the meal in their cage about a half hour before they usually wake up. You should remove any leftovers, along with the food dishes in the morning once your glider has gone to sleep. A good rule of thumb is never to leave their food in the cage for more than twelve hours.

You should provide fresh, clean water for your gliders at all times. It is a good idea to use filtered or bottled water because tap water contains chlorine, minerals, and bacteria. Some areas have better tap water than others, but it is better to be safe than sorry. It is not recommended to give them distilled water.

I am going to go over the main components of a sugar glider's diet, and then I will discuss some of the different diets that you can follow.

Protein

Your sugar gliders diet should consist of roughly 50% protein. There are a wide variety of proteins to choose from, including live insects, lean meats, eggs, naturally cultured yogurt, and cottage cheese.

Insects are the main source of protein for sugar gliders in the wild, so they love to eat live insects such as mealworms, crickets, and grasshoppers. Never feed lightning bugs to your glider, and stay away from any bugs caught outside because they may have come into contact with pesticides.

You can get insects at pet stores, or you can start mealworm or cricket farms to raise them yourself. If you do not want to deal with live insects, you can also get canned or freeze dried insects, but it is more enriching for gliders to tap into their predatory instincts to catch the live ones. It can be very entertaining to watch as your glider pounces and devours its prey.

It is a good idea to get gut-loaded mealworms and crickets for added nutrients. You can get them gut loaded from most pet stores, or you can feed the insects a high calcium diet yourself to make sure they are gut loaded before feeding them to your gliders. You can also sprinkle calcium powder over the insects if you need to add more calcium to your glider's diet.

It might not be ideal for everyone to feed live insects such as crickets, because they can get loose in your house and can also be quite messy. Gliders will spit out the cricket's heads and legs, so it has the potential to gross some people out.

Mealworms can be less of a mess to deal with, so that might be a better option for some people. However, crickets are higher in protein, lower in fat, and have a better calcium to phosphorous ratio than mealworms.

You can also feed sugar gliders frozen pinky mice, but again, this is not for everyone. Depending on how your glider eats, there may or may not be any remains left over. If you are the kind of person who does not want to deal with the leftovers, you can stick to other sources of protein.

Some other good sources of protein besides insects are lean meats, eggs, yogurt, and cottage cheese.

Lean meats are good sources of protein, but always make sure that the meat is unseasoned. Onions and garlic are toxic to gliders, and you should also avoid salt. If you have leftover meat from your own meals, make sure it does not have any seasonings, salt, or sauce on it before giving to your gliders.

Skinless and boneless white meat chicken or turkey are good lean meats to use, and you can also occasionally give your gliders lean beef, pork, or shrimp if you have it on hand. Avoid ham because it has a high salt content.

You can cook meat for your gliders in a variety of ways, including baking, boiling, broiling, and grilling. Never fry meat in butter or oil. Although you should not use seasonings, you can add flavor in other ways. You can try boiling meat in apple juice or baking it with a little bit of honey. Cut meat up into small pieces or even mince it to serve to your gliders.

Eggs are another good source of protein for gliders. You can hard boil, scramble, or even mix in some vegetables to make an omelette. You can also use whole eggs, including the shell, in blended mixtures. Egg shells are high in calcium and contain almost no phosphorous.

It should be noted that meat and eggs are high in phosphorous, so you have to be sure to balance them out with calcium-rich foods.

Naturally cultured yogurt and cottage cheese are also good sources of protein. Generally, dairy products are not good for gliders, but cottage cheese is low in lactose and the culturing process in yogurt makes lactose more digestible.

Some people feed gliders tofu, but there is some debate as to whether or not it is a good food for gliders. Soy products may have an adverse affect on the digestive system and may inhibit the absorption of nutrients.

Although gliders love nuts, you should only give one or two occasionally because they are fatty and high in phosphorous. Gliders can eat walnuts, almonds, pecans, hazelnuts, and pine nuts. You can also give sunflower seeds shelled or unshelled as a treat. Just remember only to give nuts and seeds sparingly as treats, and make sure they are raw and unsalted.

Fruits and Vegetables

Your sugar glider's diet should consist of roughly 25% fruits and 25% vegetables. You can use fresh or frozen fruits and vegetables, but stay away from canned fruits and vegetables because they contain too much sugar, sodium, and preservatives.

Dried fruit is not recommended if it contains added sugar. Also, remember that gliders are sap suckers, so they like to suck out the juice from fruit. If you dry fruit yourself or find dried fruit with no additives, you can offer it as occasional treats, but it should not make a main part of the diet.

Make sure to rinse all fruits and vegetables thoroughly to get rid of any pesticides. Also make sure to remove any pits or seeds from fruits such as apples, cherries or peaches. You can cut up fruits and vegetables into pieces your glider can hold, or you can blend them up and freeze them in ice trays to make convenient portions that can be thawed as needed.

You should offer a wide variety of fruits and vegetables for nutritional balance. Keep offering things that your glider does not like, because they change their minds. They might like something one day and ignore it the next day. Just because they did not eat something one time does not mean they will not eat it another time, so you just have to keep trying. You can also try cutting up fruits and vegetables into smaller pieces to see if your gliders prefer that.

Sometimes it may appear that your glider did not eat something, but if you check the inside, you will see that it is hollowed out. For example, gliders will often eat the inside of peas and leave the outer shell.

In choosing your fruits and vegetables, it is very important to pay attention to the calcium to phosphorous ratio. The goal is to achieve an overall calcium to phosphorous ratio of 2:1. Below are charts of some common fruits and vegetables and their corresponding calcium to phosphorous ratios. Something with a very low calcium to phosphorous, such as corn (.02:1) is something you would want to limit or avoid.

Fruit	Ca:P Ratio
Papaya	4.8:1
Figs	2.5:1
Orange	2.3:1
Kumquats	2.3:1
Raspberries	1.8:1
Blackberries	1.5:1
Grapefruit (white)	1.5:1
Tangerines	1.4:1

Grapes	1.4:1
Grapefruit (pink and red)	1.2:1
Apple (with skin)	1.1:1
Pears	1.1:1
Pineapple	1.0:1
Mango	.9:1
Melon	.9:1
Watermelon	.9:1
Cherries	.8:1
Dates	.8:1
Apricots	.7:1
Cranberries	.7:1
Kiwi	.7:1
Prunes	.7:1
Strawberries	.7:1
Apple (without skin)	.6:1
Blueberries	.6:1
Cantaloupe	.6:1
Honeydew	.6:1
Raisins	.5:1
Peaches	.4:1
Plum	.4:1
Bananas	.3:1
Nectarine	.3:1
Starfruit (Carambola)	.2:1

Vegetables	Ca:P Ratio
Collard Greens	14.5:1
Mustard Spinach	7.5:1
Turnip Greens	4.5:1
Parsley (dried)	4.2:1
Beet Greens	3.0:1
Chinese Cabbage	2.8:1
Dandelion Greens	2.8:1
Loose Leaf Lettuce	2.7:1
Kale	2.4:1
Mustard Greens	2.4:1
Parsley (fresh)	2.3:1
Chicory Greens	2.1:1
Green Cabbage	2.0:1
Spinach	2.0:1
Watercress	2.0:1
Endive	1.9:1
Spaghetti Squash	1.9:1
Leeks	1.7:1
Celery	1.5:1
Napa Cabbage	1.5:1
Butternut Squash	1.5:1
Cilantro/Coriander	1.4:1
Butterhead Lettuce	1.4:1
Okra	1.3:1
Red Cabbage	1.2:1

Radish	1.2:1
Green Beans	1.1:1
Swiss Chard	1.1:1
Tofu	1.1:1
Turnips	1.1:1
Iceberg Lettuce	1.1:1
Soybean	1.1:1
Winter Squash	1.1:1
Acorn Squash	.9:1
Romaine Lettuce	.8:1
Sweet Potato	.8:1
Broccoli	.7:1
Cucumber	.7:1
Brussel Sprouts	.6:1
Carrots	.6:1
Summer Squash	.6:1
Alfalfa Sprouts	.5:1
Asparagus	.5:1
Cauliflower	.5:1
Parsnips	.5:1
Sweet Peppers	.5:1
Pumpkin	.5:1
Zucchini	.5:1
Beets	.4:1
Avocado	.3:1
Eggplant	.3:1
Yams	.3:1

Artichoke	.2:1
Peas	.2:1
Tomato	.2:1
Corn	.02:1
Mushrooms	.02:1

Oxalic Acid

Oxalic acid binds with calcium and forms calcium oxalate, which is an insoluble salt. This means that the calcium cannot be absorbed and used by the body. Some vegetables that contain oxalic acid are spinach, rhubarb, beets, beet greens, swiss chard, celery stalks, mustard greens, kale, parsley, collard greens, turnip greens, and some beans.

You must take this into consideration when looking at the calcium content of these vegetables. Although many of these vegetables have a good calcium to phosphorous ratio, the oxalic acid will render much of the calcium unusable.

Calcium and Vitamin Supplements

If your glider eats a lot of foods that are high in phosphorous, you may need to use a calcium supplement to achieve a calcium to phosphorous ratio of 2:1. Rep-Cal makes a calcium supplement that is phosphorous free and can be sprinkled over their food. Never mix supplements in their water.

Rep-Cal also makes a multivitamin called Herptivite that can be given to gliders, but it is better to try to feed them a nutritionally balanced diet naturally. Overdoing vitamin supplements can cause liver damage and other health problems.

If you follow a diet that calls for a multivitamin supplement, that is fine because it is included in the diet plan. However, make sure to follow the diet as it is written so you do not end up overdosing on vitamins.

Foods to Avoid

There are some foods that can harm your glider and some foods that are best to avoid. Here is a list of some of the common foods that are known to be bad for sugar gliders:

- Catnip
- Wild Insects
- Lightning Bugs
- House plants
- Onion or Onion Powder
- Garlic or Garlic Powder
- Chives
- Leeks
- Scallions
- Chocolate
- Dairy (milk, cheese, butter, etc.)
- Processed Sugar
- Artificial Sweeteners

Aflatoxin

Some people avoid crickets because they can carry aflatoxin, which is fatal to gliders. Aflatoxin comes from mold which can contaminate grains such as corn. Corn-based bedding is often used in raising crickets, and this is how crickets can ingest the aflatoxin and become a carrier.

If you want to feed your glider crickets, just be aware of this issue and make sure your crickets come from a source that does not use corn-based bedding. Same goes for mealworms, which can also be contaminated if they are kept in corn-based bedding.

Aflatoxin can potentially contaminate peanuts, pellets, and other foods as well. Be careful when storing foods to make sure no moisture can get in, and freeze pellets to keep them fresh. Discard any leftover food in your glider's cage each morning and make sure to wash out food dishes to prevent mold from forming.

Established Diets

There are many acceptable diets that sugar glider breeders and owners have developed over the years. You can choose to follow one of these diets or you can feed your glider a well balanced diet of 2 tablespoons of protein, 1 tablespoon of fruits, and 1 tablespoon of vegetables, making sure to provide a variety of each.

If you choose to use an established diet, you should follow the diet exactly as it is written unless otherwise instructed. These diets usually have already taken into account the proper calcium to phosphorous ratio, so changing the ingredients can throw off the ratio.

Here is a list of some popular diets. Visit the websites provided for more information on each diet.

High Protein Wombaroo (HPW)

HPW was created by Peggy Brewer and is a very popular diet among sugar glider owners. There are two exotic ingredients in this diet that must be specially ordered: the High Protein Wombaroo powder and the bee pollen. You can read more about this diet here: http://www.sweet-sugar-gliders.com/sugar-glider-hpw-diet-high-protein-wombaroo-recipe.html.

Bourbon's Modified Leadbeater's (BML)

BML is a modification of the Leadbeater's Diet that was developed by the Taronga Zoo in Sydney, Australia. This is also a very popular diet used by sugar glider owners. You can read more about this diet here: http://www.sweet-sugar-gliders.com/original-bml-diet-bourbons-modified-leadbeaters-recipe.html.

Priscilla's Diet/Pet Glider Nutrition System/Pet Glider Exotic Diet

Priscilla's Diet, the Pet Glider Nutrition System, and the Pet Glider Exotic Diet all refer to the same diet that was created by Priscilla Price at The Pet Glider. She has used this diet for over a thousand sugar gliders successfully, including gliders that needed rehabilitation. You can read more about this diet here: http://www.thepetglider.com/the-pet-glider-nutrition-system.html.

Suncoast Diet

This diet is used by Suncoast Sugar Gliders and was developed by a veterinarian they work with. You can read more about this diet here: http://www.sugar-gliders.com/sugar-glider-diet.htm.

LGRS Suggie Soup

This is the diet that is used for rescues that are rehabilitated at the Lucky Glider Rescue and Sanctuary. You can read more about this diet here: http://www.sugarglider.com/gliderpedia/index.asp?LGRSSuggieSoup.

HPW Plus and HPW Complete

These are two new diets developed by Peggy Brewer, the creator of the HPW diet. She created these new diets in response to concerns that the calcium to phosphorous ratio in the HPW diet was too low, as well as problems obtaining the High Protein Wombaroo Powder from Australia.

She worked with a team of nutritionists, chemists, and veterinarians to develop these new products. The HPW Plus is a powder that requires other ingredients to be added, while HPW Complete is an all in one powder that just requires water to be added. You can read more about these diets here: http://www.hpwdietcenter.com.

Chapter 7: Health

To keep your glider healthy, you should provide a nutritionally balanced diet, keep its environment clean, give it plenty of time to play outside of the cage, and prevent stressful or hazardous situations. Most health issues arise as a result of a poor diet and can be avoided.

Finding A Veterinarian

It is important to find a veterinarian and an emergency clinic before you get your sugar glider. You will need to call and ask if the veterinarian takes sugar gliders as patients. It is also a good idea to ask whether the veterinarian has experience treating sugar gliders. It is best to find somebody who is familiar with sugar gliders and already has experience treating them.

If your veterinarian is not available for emergencies, then you will need to find an emergency clinic that treats sugar gliders. It is very important to find an emergency clinic and make sure that you have the phone number and location readily accessible. In times of an emergency, you do not want to waste time trying to find a clinic that accepts sugar gliders because it could mean the difference between the life and death of your glider.

You will need to take your sugar glider in for an annual wellness exam. The first exam should take place within two weeks of getting your sugar glider to make sure your glider is healthy. Make sure to keep a copy of your sugar glider's medical records after each veterinarian visit. In an emergency, it is helpful to have these records on hand.

One thing to remember is never to let a veterinarian float or file your sugar glider's teeth. If a veterinarian is inexperienced with sugar gliders, they may assume that they are like rodents and need to have their teeth trimmed. However, sugar gliders teeth do not continue to grow, so it will cause permanent pain and difficulty eating if their teeth are trimmed.

Watch For Signs Because Sugar Gliders Hide Illnesses

It is important to know that sugar gliders instinctively hide illness until they are extremely sick or near death. In the wild, a sick sugar glider will be rejected by other members of the colony because the weak glider would attract predators.

Because of their natural instinct to hide illness for as long as they can, even the smallest and seemingly insignificant changes in mood or behavior can be a red flag that something is wrong. Unfortunately, if you do not monitor your glider's behavior closely, by the time you notice any sign of illness, it may be too late.

For this reason, it is important to bond with your glider and get to know its habits, moods, and sleeping patterns. The better you get to know your glider, the more you will be able to notice the subtle changes that can indicate illness. If something seems off or your glider is behaving abnormally, you should see a veterinarian immediately.

Here is a list of signs and symptoms to watch out for that may indicate your glider has a serious health problem. If you notice any changes in your gliders appearance or behavior, even if they are not included in this list, you should see a veterinarian immediately.

Signs Of Illness:

- Limping or dragging legs, especially the back legs or hindquarters
- Curling or swollen feet or toes
- Trembling, shaking, or shivering violently or for prolonged periods of time
- Moving slowly or not moving at all
- Wobbling, uncoordinated movements, jerkiness, falling over, muscle spasms, or seizures
- Frantic climbing or any other spastic movements that may be a fear response
- Any injuries, including cuts, punctures, fractures,

dislocations, unusually angled joints, or a disjointed tail
- Any visible wounds or raw-looking areas
- Droopy or flattened ears
- Blackened or crusty ears
- Dull eyes that lack luster or cloudy eyes
- Nose, ears, or feet change color from healthy pink to pale/whitish, blue/purple, dark red, or yellowish color
- Discharge from eyes or nose
- Swelling, lumps, or protrusions
- Blackened/necrotic tissue
- Sudden weight gain or loss
- Vomiting
- Tilting head or loss of balance
- Paws at face or head in a way that is not normal grooming behavior
- Fur looks wet on the throat, neck, and tummy
- Not grooming or fur clumped together
- Thinning fur, bald spots, or dull fur that has lost its luster
- Change in body temperature; may feel cold to the touch
- Change in sleeping pattern, such as staying awake during the day or oversleeping
- Refusing to eat or drink
- Excessive thirst
- Skin between shoulder blades tents and does not return to normal when you pinch it
- Not urinating or defecating
- Sudden change in color, smell, or consistency of urine or feces
- Hisses while defecating or urinating or other signs of painful defecation or urination
- Fast or labored breathing, or a popping/clicking sound while breathing (Some gliders make this sound while they are sleeping, but if they make this

sound with every breath while they are awake, it could be a sign of respiratory problems such as pneumonia.)

- Swollen jaw
- Using back teeth to bite rather than the front teeth
- Other gliders suddenly attack when they used to get along
- Change in mood or temperament, sudden aggression

If you notice any of the symptoms listed here, you should take your glider to the veterinarian immediately. Do not try to diagnose and treat the problem yourself. A veterinarian can perform necessary testing and give you a more accurate diagnosis and course of treatment.

I will go over some of the health problems that can arise with sugar gliders. Again, if you suspect your sugar glider is sick, you should get veterinary care for your glider immediately. The following is provided as general educational information and is not meant to replace a proper medical diagnosis.

Calcium Deficiency

There are several terms that may be used to describe this condition, including Calcium Deficiency, Metabolic Bone Disease (MBD), Hind Leg Paralysis (HLP), Nutritional Secondary Hyperparathyroidism, Nutritional Osteodystrophy, and Hypocalcemia. There are subtle differences in the technicalities of these terms, but for practical purposes, you can group them together.

Calcium Deficiency can result from a poor diet, but it can also be caused by a bacterial or parasitic infection. If caught early and treated properly, this condition can be reversed and your sugar glider can live a healthy life.

Nutritionally, Calcium Deficiency can be caused by a lack of calcium in the diet or too much phosphorous in the diet, which inhibits calcium absorption. A Vitamin D deficiency or excessive fat intake can also inhibit the absorption of calcium.

Even if you feed your glider a proper diet, it is very important to see a veterinarian immediately if your glider shows any signs of Calcium Deficiency. Calcium Deficiency is not only caused by a poor diet. It can also be a symptom of a bacterial or parasitic infection, which interferes with the normal absorption of calcium or leaches calcium from the bones. When it is the result of a bacterial or parasitic infection, the symptoms can develop very quickly.

Signs of Calcium Deficiency include lethargy, weakness, lack of appetite or sudden weight loss, dizziness, shaking or trembling, muscle spasms or seizures, limping, dragging one or both hind legs, difficulty walking or climbing, difficulty gripping, uncoordinated movements, paralysis, swollen toes, swollen or stiff joints, and bone fractures.

If you notice any of these symptoms, take your glider to a veterinarian immediately. Even gliders who have severe symptoms can make a full recovery if treated promptly.

It is important to get a veterinarian diagnosis to determine whether your glider actually has a Calcium Deficiency. They usually use bone x-rays to make a diagnosis. It is also important to determine the cause of the condition. If symptoms came on gradually, it is most likely the result of a nutritional imbalance. If symptoms appeared quickly, testing should be done to check for bacterial or parasitic infections.

Your veterinarian will determine the proper course of treatment. In most cases, you will administer an oral calcium supplement for a period of time and make adjustments to your sugar glider's diet. In some cases, your veterinarian may administer calcium injections. You will need to go to follow up appointments so your veterinarian can continue to monitor your glider's progress.

Dehydration

Dehydration is usually a symptom of an underlying health problem. While it is important to treat the dehydration right away, you should also see a veterinarian immediately to determine the cause of dehydration.

You can perform a "tent test" to determine whether your sugar glider is dehydrated. Gently pull up the skin between the shoulder blades, and if the skin stays tented for more than a few seconds, the glider is dehydrated. The longer it stays tented, the more dehydrated the glider.

You can use a needless syringe to feed your glider unflavored Pedialyte. If you do not have unflavored Pedialyte on hand, use regular water instead. You can cradle your glider on its back in your hand and bring the syringe lightly to its mouth. Gently squeeze out a drop onto its lips until your glider starts licking. Be gentle and do not squeeze too much out at one time. If liquid is forced down into your gliders mouth, it can aspirate into the lungs.

It is important to see a veterinarian as soon as possible. If your glider is severely dehydrated, the veterinarian may need to administer fluids by subcutaneous injection.

Obesity

Obesity is a common health problem for sugar gliders in captivity. They are tiny creatures, so it is easy to overfeed them without realizing it. They also love foods that are high in sugar and fat, so it may be tempting to feed them too much of the treats that they love.

Obesity is a serious health risk that can lead to numerous health problems. It can cause fat deposits to build up in the eyes, lethargy, and problems with the heart, liver, kidney, and pancreas. Obesity is a serious problem and will generally decrease the life span of your sugar glider.

In the wild, sugar gliders have to work for their food and they burn a lot of calories in the process. In captivity, sugar gliders can easily become obese, so you must maintain a healthy diet and make sure they get enough exercise.

You should consult with your veterinarian to determine what a suitable weight is for your sugar glider. All sugar gliders are built differently, so there is no universally accepted weight. Your veterinarian should also advise you on how to adjust your glider's diet. You will most likely need to cut back on fatty foods. If you give your glider honey, it is high in calories and can contribute to obesity.

Some gliders may get enough exercise and eat a balanced diet, but they just overeat. You will have to control portions for these gliders and may need to feed them separately if you have more than one glider.

To ensure that your gliders get enough exercise, you should provide them with an exercise wheel. I recommend the Stealth Wheel. You can get the stealth wheel here: http://www.atticworx.com.

You should also make sure the cage is big enough. If a cage is too small, your gliders will not have enough room to keep up a normal activity level and they will not burn enough calories.

Underweight

Sugar gliders may be underweight for various reasons. They may not be getting enough calories in their diet or they may not be absorbing nutrients. They could also have parasites or another type of illness that causes weight loss. Stress is another factor that can cause weight loss. Since weight loss can be a symptom of an underlying health issue, you should take your glider to a veterinarian to be checked out.

If you have more than one glider, there may be an issue with one glider eating the other glider's share of the food. If this is the case, you should set up two feeding stations to make sure the underweight glider receives enough food.

Diarrhea

Diarrhea can have many different causes, including stress, eating too much citrus or dairy, gastroenteritis, eating toxic substances, eating food contaminated by aflatoxin, bacterial or viral infections, or parasites.

Tapeworms, roundworms, hookworms, and giardia are all intestinal parasites that can cause diarrhea. It is important to wash all fruits and vegetables thoroughly because they may be contaminated by parasites. You should also be sure to wash your hands before handling your glider's food, food bowls, toys, and cage.

Diarrhea can quickly lead to dehydration, so it is vital to address the problem right away. There will often be an underlying cause that needs to be treated, so you should see a veterinarian as soon as possible.

Constipation

Sugar gliders can become constipated for different reasons, but it is usually related to their diet. Signs of constipation include straining or hissing while defecating, dry, hard stools, a distended abdomen or hard mass in the belly, or no bowl movements for 24 hours.

If your glider is constipated, you can try correcting it on your own. If it does not improve within 24 hours, you should see a veterinarian as soon as possible. Constipation can be very painful for your glider and can eventually lead to death if left untreated.

There are several foods you can give your glider to help alleviate constipation. A very small amount of canned pumpkin works well. Make sure it is real pumpkin and not pumpkin pie mix. Raisins, figs, prunes, peach or apricot nectar, or diluted apple juice may also help.

Dental/Periodontal

Sugar gliders can get periodontal disease and tooth abscesses. It is a good idea to inspect your gliders teeth and gums at least once a month to look for signs of trouble. You should also have your veterinarian check your glider's periodontal health during annual wellness checks.

Some signs of periodontal disease include swelling of the face or jaw, difficulty eating certain foods, sudden weight loss, decreased activity, changes in behavior, red or bleeding gums, tartar on the teeth, and missing or loose teeth.

Some of the symptoms of periodontal disease may also be indicative of other health problems, so it is important to have a veterinarian check out your glider to be sure what the problem is.

Sugar gliders can also develop tooth abscesses which may be related to an underlying issue of periodontal disease. A tooth abscess forms when there is a bacterial infection in the center of a tooth. It will usually show up as a swollen area on the upper or lower jaw and may make a glider's eye puff or bulge out.

If your glider has a tooth abscess, you need to see a veterinarian immediately to drain the abscess and get antibiotics. You may also have to extract the tooth to take care of the underlying problem. Tooth abscesses are very painful and are life threatening if left untreated.

Stress and Depression

Sugar gliders can suffer from stress and even depression just like humans. Gliders are more likely to get sick when they are stressed or depressed because their immune systems are not as strong. All gliders have different personalities and react to stress in different ways. For this reason, it is important to get know your glider's behaviors and habits well so you can spot changes and abnormal behaviors.

There are many different sources of stress for gliders. Moving to a new home, adding a cage mate, or losing a cage mate are all potential sources of stress for gliders. Some other causes of stress include a poor diet, unsanitary living conditions, illness, a small cage, other household pets, loneliness, and boredom.

Some signs to look for that indicate stress are overeating or under eating, lethargy or inactivity, eating their own feces, grumpiness, crabbing, barking, crying, hissing, aggression, pacing or circling repeatedly, change in sleep pattern, over grooming, and self-mutilation.

Single gliders are prone to depression and may over groom or self-mutilate if you don't spend enough time with them. It is much better to have more than one glider because they really need the companionship of their own kind.

If your glider shows signs of stress or depression, you should see a veterinarian immediately. Stressed gliders often have underlying illnesses that may have caused your glider to become stressed in the first place. On the other hand, stressed gliders are more prone to developing illnesses. It is not always possible to know which came first, the stress or the illness, but it is important to treat the illness as soon as possible.

Self-Mutilation

When a sugar glider chews on its own body, it is referred to as self-mutilation. Although rare, it is life threatening, so it is something glider owners should be aware of and prepared for in case it does happen.

A self-mutilating glider basically feels as though it is being attacked by an invisible enemy. They feel pain or discomfort and react by attacking back to try to remove the pain. Sugar gliders may self-mutilate in response to an injury, infection, illness, or stress.

Some self-mutilating gliders, but not all, make a distinctive noise before or during self-mutilation. This noise sounds like a crabbing or hissing sound, similar to the noise gliders make while fighting with each other, but it has a pained quality to it. It is a very alarming sound, and if you ever hear it, you will definitely know something is wrong.

Self mutilation of the tail, feet, or toes is typically a result of an injury or infection, while self mutilation of the abdomen, cloaca, or base of the tail is usually a result of an infection. Self-mutilation of the abdomen, cloaca, or base of the tail can be fatal in as little as an hour, so it is vital to act quickly in these cases.

If your glider is self-mutilating, you need to put an e-collar on immediately to prevent further damage. You can find instructions on how to make an e-collar here: http://www.suzsugargliders.com/ecollar.htm. If you would rather buy an e-collar, you can purchase one here: http://www.thegliderinitiative.org/tgistore.htm.

Next, you will need to get your glider to a veterinarian as soon as possible to get a diagnosis. Once you are able to treat the problem and your glider is healed again, you can remove the e-collar. However, once a glider has self-mutilated, it is at risk of self-mutilating again in the future if it gets another infection or injury. You will always need to watch these gliders closely for the remainder of their lives.

Setting Up A Hospital Cage

You can set up a smaller travel size cage or 38 gallon reptarium to serve as a hospital cage for a sick glider. A hospital cage is basically just a smaller cage that allows you to confine a sick glider who may have a hard time getting around a bigger cage.

A hospital cage can serve two main purposes. First, it allows a sick glider easy access to its pouch, food, and water. Second, if you have more than one glider, it allows you to separate the sick glider from its cage mates.

Emergency Medical Kit

It is a good idea to have a medical kit handy in case of an emergency. If your glider is seriously ill, having supplies on hand could help save its life. You can purchase a ready-made emergency medical kit here: http://www.thegliderinitiative.org/tgistore.htm or put it together yourself with the following recommended items.

- Emergency Phone Numbers and Addresses
- Map and Directions to Emergency Clinic
- E-Collar
- Moleskin (for padding the edges of the e-collar)
- 1 cc and 3 cc Needless Syringes Plus Feeding Tips

(for force feeding and medicating)
- Wombaroo Marsupial Milk Replacer or Ebsilac Puppy Formula (for force feeding)
- Unflavored Pedialyte (for dehydration)
- Q-Tips (for cleaning wounds and applying topical medications)
- Cotton Balls (for cleaning wounds)
- Gauze (for dressing wounds)
- Self-Adhering Bandage Wrap or Veterinarian Tape (for wrapping wounds)
- Neosporin (antibiotic for treating wounds)*
- QuickDerm (for treating wounds)
- Sterile 0.9 Saline Solution (for cleaning wounds)
- Sensitive Eyes Saline Solution (for flushing eyes)
- Styptic Powder (for treating bleeding nails)
- Nail Clippers or Cuticle Clippers (for trimming nails)
- Small Scissors
- Tweezers
- Hand Warmers or Heating Pad (for keeping a sick glider warm if necessary)
- Large Fleece Blankets Stored in Airtight Bag (for wrapping up a sick glider and keeping it warm)
- Pouch or Carrier (for traveling to veterinarian or emergency clinic)

*Neosporin can be toxic if ingested, so it is advised to use it in conjunction with an e-collar. Neosporin Plus Pain Relief should only be used on a glider in an e-collar because it has a numbing effect and could numb a glider's tongue and mouth if licked

Chapter 8: Hygiene

P racticing good hygiene is very important to keep your sugar gliders healthy. You will need to keep your glider's environment clean, but sugar gliders are very good at keeping themselves clean. Sugar gliders groom themselves and do a very good job, so you do not need to worry about giving them baths.

However, if something were to spill on them that they could not clean off themselves, you could wipe it off with a wet cloth or rinse it off with some warm water and just pat dry. Make sure they are kept warm while they are drying off, but never try using a blow dryer on them because it would scare them.

One thing you may need to do for glider is keep their nails trimmed. In the wild, gliders nails naturally get filed down by the rough bark on trees, but in captivity, they can grow to be too sharp. If their nails are too sharp, it will hurt when they climb on you because their nails will puncture your skin.

It can also be harmful to your glider if their nails are too sharp because they can get snagged on their pouch or other fabrics they come into contact with. If your glider's nail does get caught on something, it may panic and struggle to get free which can cause injuries. The worst case scenario is that a glider may actually chew its own toe or foot off to get free.

You can use regular nail clippers or cuticle clippers to trim their nails. You only want to trim the very tip off while being very careful not to trim into the quick of the nail, which is the vein that grows in the nail. The nails will bleed if you trim them too short, so make sure to have some styptic powder on hand to stop the bleeding. You can also use cornstarch or flour to stop the bleeding.

Another reason you want to make sure not to trim the nails too short is that it can inhibit your glider's ability to climb and hold onto things.

Another thing to be aware of is that you should only trim the two outermost nails of your gliders back feet. It is not recommended to trim the nails on their two toes that are fused together because those toes are used as a grooming comb, and the thumbs on their feet do not have nails at all. All five nails on their hands should be trimmed.

It may be difficult to trim your glider's nails. You can try wrapping your glider up in a blanket like a burrito and keep one foot out. When you are done trimming those nails, allow your glider to pull the foot back in and try pulling another foot out. Make sure to give your glider some treats during the process and afterwards as a reward.

You can also try an alternative method such as the Trim Trax that can be purchased with the Stealth Wheel. The Trim Trax can be used to maintain nails once they have already been trimmed.

Keeping Your Sugar Glider's Environment Clean

It is important to keep your glider's environment clean for their overall health and well-being, as well as to keep odors to a minimum. There are several different approaches to cleaning, so you will have to determine what works best for you. It is good to form a habit or cleaning cycle that you follow regularly so there is some consistency for your glider.

Generally, there are two kinds of cleaning that should be done. There are major cage cleanings, and then there are the cage wipe-downs or spot cleanings that you do in between major cleanings.

Some people do major cleanings once a month, every other month, or every three months. How often you need to do a major cleaning will really depend on how often you spot clean, how messy your glider is, and how much your glider marks the cage.

For major cleanings, you can take your cage outside and hose it down or use a pressure washer. If you cannot take it outside, try washing it in a bathtub.

For disinfecting your cage during major cleanings, you can use a bleach and water solution. Make sure to rinse off all the bleach and if you can, let it dry in direct sunlight to decompose any remaining bleach residue. A little bit of dawn dish soap in water also works well to remove built up food and gunk from the cage.

If you want to use natural cleaning products, you can use a vinegar and water solution. Just make sure never to mix vinegar and bleach because it creates toxic fumes. Steam cleaners may also be a good alternative to chemical cleaners.

Some people do not like to do complete cage cleanings and choose to clean in stages or sections. The reasoning for this is that some gliders will mark a cage more after it has been completely cleaned because it no longer smells right to them.

You should also be spot cleaning or wiping down the cage bars in between major cleanings. This will not only help keep the cage clean, but it will also help control odors. While you will not be able to eliminate odors completely, there is a lot you can do to keep it under control.

Sugar gliders can be messy eaters, and they also poop and pee wherever they need to. Bacteria that builds up from food splatters, urine, and feces is what tends to create the most odor. Sugar gliders themselves do have an odor, but it is mainly the un-neutered males that have the strongest odor. Un-neutered males have a strong, musky scent, and their urine smells stronger as well.

If you want to keep odors to a minimum, you should make it a habit to wipe up any food spills, remove fecal droppings, and do a quick wipe-down of the cage bars for urine. It really goes a long way to keep odors from getting out of control.

Cage wipe-downs only take a couple of minutes, so try to do it every morning if you can. If you cannot do daily wipe-downs, just try to do them as often as you can. It is also important to change out drop pan bedding daily or every other day to reduce odors.

For cage wipe-downs, clorox wipes work well. They do not contain bleach and are safe for sugar gliders. They may leave a sticky residue, so it's not a bad idea to wipe the bars with warm water afterwards. You can also use a vinegar and water solution, or just wet a paper towel or wash cloth with warm water for the wipe-downs.

In addition to cleaning the cage, you will also need to keep your gliders food and water dishes, toys, and pouches clean. Food and water dishes should be cleaned every morning when you remove any leftover food from the night before.

You can keep several sets of toys and and pouches so they can be rotated for cleaning. Pouches should be laundered weekly, and toys should be rotated for cleaning weekly as well. To clean toys and exercise wheels, soak them in soapy water or scrub them with a brush. If you give your glider natural climbing branches, make sure to replace them if they get soiled.

Chapter 9: Bonding

Since sugar gliders are social animals, they will form a strong bond to their owners. Bonding is one of the things people often have questions about, because it does not always happen easily. I will address some of the most common questions about bonding throughout this section.

There are many factors that can determine how the bonding process goes. The personality of your glider will have an affect on the bonding process. All gliders have unique personalities, so you will have to get to know your individual glider and adjust your behavior accordingly.

The age of your glider may also have an affect on how quickly you will be able to bond. It is usually easier to bond with joeys, but it is possible to bond with gliders of any age. It may take more time to bond with older gliders, but any glider can be bonded to a human if the human makes the commitment to do so.

Another factor that affects bonding is where your glider came from and whether they were handled by humans. It is better to get your glider from a breeder who handles their gliders so they are not afraid of human handling. The glider will still need to get used to you, but it will probably be easier to bond with a glider that is already used to human handling.

Finally, one of the most important factors that affects the bonding process is your own attitude. It is necessary to be loving, patient, and persistent during the process. If you make a commitment to take whatever time is necessary to bond with your glider, it will truly pay off. Once your glider has bonded to you, they make the most wonderful and loyal pets.

How Long Does Bonding Take?

One common question people have about bonding is how long it should take. There is no single answer to this question because all gliders are different. If your glider is already used to being handled by humans and does not have a natural fear towards you, it may bond to you almost immediately. That is not common, so consider yourself very lucky if it happens to you!

In some very extreme cases, it could take years to form a bond with a glider. This is more likely in the case where a glider was abused by its previous owner and had formed a strong fear of humans.

In most cases, it will take about a month, and possibly up to three to five months to bond with a glider.

The bonding process happens in stages, so the bond can continue to grow and become stronger over the years. You should be prepared to commit at least a month to the bonding process, and keep in mind that it may take a little bit longer.

How To Initiate The Bonding Process

The two most important things to understand about gliders is that they bond by scent and are territorial by nature. Gliders recognize the members of its own colony by their scent, and they will attack or even kill gliders that approach from other colonies and are marked with another scent.

When you bring a glider to a new home, the change in environment can be very stressful. You will need to give them a few days to get used to their new surroundings and become familiar with all the new sights, sounds, and smells. It is natural for a glider to be afraid in a new environment, so you should not try to handle them during this adjustment period.

Even though you will need to give your glider time to get used to its new home, you should still initiate the bonding process right away. The first step you should take is to help your glider get used to your scent. You can do this by hanging a dirty shirt you wore the day before over the cage.

You can also tuck a small piece of fleece, about four to five square inches, into your clothing and wear it for a day. Then place the worn fleece into your glider's sleeping pouch. This little piece of fleece is known as a "bonding blanket." Your glider will love to snuggle up to it in its pouch and it will also get used to your scent.

Once your glider gets used to your scent, try not to change any products you use, such as soap, hand lotion, deodorant, or cologne. Changes in scent can confuse your glider and make you seem like a stranger.

In the first few days, you can also sit near the cage and speak to your glider to help it get used to your presence. Speak in a soothing voice and let your glider know you are a friend. You can also try offering treats through the cage bars so your glider starts to associate you with positive things.

Wearing Your Sugar Glider During The Day

Once you have given your glider a few days to get used to its new home, you can try wearing it on you during the day while it is inside its pouch. You can get a pouch that is specifically for bonding, or you can use the same pouch it sleeps in. It may be easier to wait until your glider goes into the pouch to sleep, and then remove the pouch from the cage and wear it around your neck, close to your heart.

Some people wear two shirts and tuck the pouch in between. For ladies, if you can find a tank top with a built in shelf bra, that also works well to support the pouch. There are also pouches that have straps to go around your shoulders and waist to secure the pouch close to you and prevent it from swinging around.

When you transfer your pouch from the cage, your glider may crab at you. This sound is loud and can be alarming, but do not pull back. It is important not to let your glider intimidate you. The crabbing is a defensive sound and just means your glider is afraid. You can gently stroke your glider through the pouch and assure it in a soothing voice that everything is okay.

During the day while you are wearing your glider, speak to your glider and offer it small treats, such as a piece of fruit. Do not reach in, just hold the treat at the opening of the pouch and wait until your glider pokes out and let it take the treat on its own. You can pet your glider through the pouch and when it becomes more comfortable with you, you can try reaching in to pet it every now and then.

You can also offer licky treats to your glider by putting a dab of honey, yogurt, or applesauce on your finger. Allowing your glider to lick it off your finger will help them trust you and associate you with good things.

When the treat has almost been licked off completely, add more to your finger or pull your finger away, because your glider might bite your finger once it is all gone. In the wild, they bite into branches to get more sap to flow out, so they might bite your finger instinctively to get more of the yummy treat.

If you are bonding with more than one glider, you should work with each glider separately. Physical separation is important so they bond with you and do not seek comfort in each other.

You can keep them in the same cage, but when you take them out during the day to bond, keep them in separate pouches. You can wear them on you at the same time as long as they are not in the same pouch together, otherwise they will attach to each other as a source of security.

It is normal for multiple gliders to bond to each other, but that does not prevent them from bonding to you as well. By separating them while you bond with them individually, you are just allowing them to form a bond with you rather than reinforcing the bond they have with each other.

You should wear your glider as much as possible to build a strong bond. If you need to leave your house, you can take them out with you during your normal daily activities.

In the early bonding stages, you should keep them secured in a zippered bonding pouch any time you take your glider out of your home. This is just an extra safety precaution so they will not escape. Once your glider has bonded to you, you may not have to keep them zipped in if you know your glider will not try to escape.

How To Pick Up Your Sugar Glider

Another common question people ask is how to pick up a glider from the cage. When it comes time to handling your glider for the first time, it is important to be confident and fearless. For the first time, try handling your glider during the day because they will be sleepy and easier to handle.

A good way to pick up a glider is to use a scooping motion with a cupped hand. Do not just reach into the cage and grab your glider because they do not like to be confined or restricted.

Approach with a treat and coax them into your cupped hand so that they are holding onto you rather than you holding onto them.

If they are holding onto the cage bars, you can approach with a cupped hand and use your finger to reach under its feet and try to coax them into holding onto you rather than the cage.

Another method is to approach your glider with a flat hand, palm facing down. You can try to place your hand underneath your glider and slide it underneath its feet. This way, you can let your glider walk onto your hand and hold onto you on its own. It's a good idea to have a treat ready as soon as your glider gets onto your hand to reinforce the behavior.

One thing to be aware of is never to grab your glider by the tail. The tail can actually come off in your hands, so it is never wise to hold them by the tail. Always make sure to handle their bodies rather than their tails.

Some gliders may react defensively when you approach. They might make the crabbing sound and get up on their back feet and stand like a bear, or they might lay on their back with their arms waving around. They may even lunge at you and try to bite you.

The most important thing is not to be afraid and not to back off. These tiny animals have the power to instill a lot of fear in people, but just remember that they cannot seriously harm you.

It is very important not to be afraid or anxious when approaching your glider, because they will sense your fear and anxiety and react by feeling scared and anxious themselves. You need to be calm and confident, and handle them gently. If you are sure-handed with them, they will feel more comfortable and trust you more easily.

If on the other hand you react to their crabbing or defensive posture by pulling away and giving up, you will reinforce their behavior. They will know that their actions will cause you to go away, so they will keep doing it when they get scared.

If you show them that you are not afraid and assure them that you are a friend, they will start to trust you. Your glider needs to feel safe with you and know that you are not intimidated by it.

If your glider bites you, it is better to take the bite calmly than to freak out and run away. I know this may sound crazy, but you will be much better off taking the bite. The more your glider realizes that you do not react to the bite, the less likely they are to try to bite you again. If they learn that they can get you to go away every time they bite you, they will keep doing it.

It usually does not hurt when a joey bites you, but adults can hurt you and even break the skin. Their bite makes a small puncture wound, so make sure to wash off your skin if it gets punctured. Fortunately, a glider bite cannot do the kind of damage that a dog bite can do, so it is not that bad.

One thing you can do to lessen the blow is hold your hand flat and taut. It is a lot harder for a glider to bite your hand that way. You can also try making a "pssst" sound whenever your glider bites, because this is the sound gliders make to each other to say "stop it!"

Bonding During Play Time

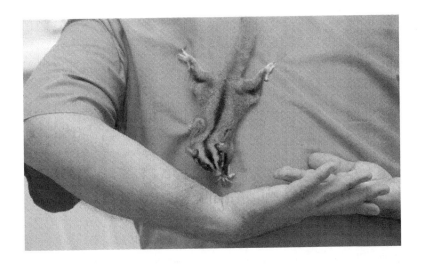

Once your glider is comfortable with you handling it, you can start to bond during play time at night. The more time you spend playing with your glider, the quicker it will bond with you.

You can let your glider out in a glider-proofed room to play with you, or some people use a small tent. You can get a small, inexpensive tent that pops up and fits easily in any room. Glider owners refer to this as "tent time."

Tent time is a good way to bond with your glider because it forces them to stay close to you. You can bring your glider in while it is still in its pouch, about a half hour before it usually wakes up. Make sure to have treats on hand and bring in some interactive toys, such as feathers.

Coax your glider out of the pouch with a treat, and let your glider explore the tent. Have fun playing and interacting with your glider inside the tent where your glider cannot get too far away. If your glider starts to interact with you, that is great progress.

If you do decide to use a tent, just make sure never to leave your glider inside unsupervised. Their nails could get caught in the seams or the windows of the tent.

If you are bonding with multiple gliders, you can play with them together as a group, or individually if you prefer. If you play with them as a group, just make sure to give each of them a little one on one attention as you interact with treats and toys.

When you are playing and interacting with your glider, it is common for them to climb on you and jump off. Their gliding membrane will spread out and they may land with a thud. It may seem like they landed too hard, but it is perfectly normal for them, so do not worry.

If you want your glider to come back, do not try to chase after it. Approach calmly with a treat and extend your hand for them to climb back on you.

How To Know When Your Sugar Glider Has Bonded To You

Spend as much time as you can playing with your glider each night and wearing it during the day. If you do this consistently for a few weeks, the bonding process should progress smoothly.

When you reach the point where your glider comes towards the cage door to greet you when you approach, that is a very good sign that your glider is bonding to you. If your glider still runs away when you approach the cage, you have some more work to do.

The more time you can spend with your glider, the more they will bond to you. Consistency is also very important during the bonding process. It helps if you can keep a routine and spend the same amount of time with them at the same time each day and night. Gliders respond well to routines and they will start to look forward to your presence.

If your glider takes a little longer to bond with you, do not worry that your glider does not like you. Some gliders are just a little more afraid of humans and take a little longer to trust us. Bonding is all about building trust, so just continue to make your glider feel safe around you and in time, it will learn to trust you.

If the bonding process does not come easily, it is important not to get discouraged. Do not try to rush things and go at your glider's pace. Be patient and trust that it will happen in time if you stay committed to the process. Your patience and determination will pay off if you keep at it.

Chapter 10: Travel

If you need to travel, it is possible to take your sugar gliders with you, or you could find somebody to take care of them while you are gone. You will need to evaluate the situation to determine whether or not it would be wise to bring them with you.

The first thing you should consider is whether your glider is used to traveling. If you take your glider out of the house often during your daily activities, then traveling with your glider should not be a problem. On the other hand if your glider has never been out of its own environment, a trip might be too stressful. In that case, you are probably better off finding somebody to take care of your glider in its own environment.

Next, you should consider how you are going to be traveling and if it will work out to have your glider come with you. If you will be driving, it would be easiest to just wear your glider. If you cannot wear your glider, make sure you will be able to secure a cage or carrier somewhere in the vehicle.

If you will be traveling by plane, you will need to check with the airline to see whether sugar gliders are allowed. You will need to make a reservation for your glider to accompany you and you will have to obtain a health certificate from a veterinarian.

Some airlines allow gliders in a carrier in the cabin, while others require that they travel in cargo. Traveling in cargo could be stressful, so it is not advised if you can avoid it. One important thing to keep in mind is that gliders need to be kept at a comfortable temperature, around 70 to 90 degrees. The cargo area of a plane may not be temperature regulated and could get too cold.

The next thing to look into is where you will be traveling and whether gliders are legal there. If gliders are not legal there, you should find somebody to take care of them rather than risk getting into trouble.

One more thing to consider is whether or not you will be able to let your gliders out of their cage for play time. If you will not have access to a glider-proofed room, you may want to bring a small tent along for play time.

If you do decide to travel with your glider, you will need to bring a travel cage. There are different sizes and styles available, including some that collapse for easy storage.

You should also try to bring along your glider's regular food to keep some consistency. If you need to refrigerate it, you can bring along a travel cooler.

If you decide to find somebody to look after your gliders while you are gone, it is best to have that person come to your place to take care of your gliders in a familiar environment. Have the sitter come over a few times to feed and play with your glider before you leave so your glider can get used to having a new person around.

If you must move your gliders to the sitter's home, do so a few days in advance so you can spend time with them in the new environment. This will help the transition to go more smoothly.

You should also help the sitter glider proof a room in his or her home where the gliders can be let out to play. Make sure to show the sitter how to prepare your gliders food, and instruct them on the proper way to handle gliders. If it is possible, you should also try to have the sitter stick to the same schedule your gliders are used to. It helps to write down all of your instructions, and also include phone numbers to your veterinarian and your emergency veterinarian.

Appendix: Resources

http://www.sugarglidercare.net

http://www.sugarglider.com

http://www.glidercentral.net

http://www.thegliderinitiative.org

http://www.sugargliderhelp.com

http://www.suzsugargliders.com

http://www.sugarglider.com/archives/ruth

http://www.sweet-sugar-gliders.com

http://www.sugarglider63.com/faqs.html

http://www.suggiesavers.org

http://www.luckyglider.org

http://www.millbreederproject.com

http://www.sugar-gliders.com

http://www.sm.all4gliders.com (self-mutilation)

Index

Made in the USA
Middletown, DE
21 February 2017